Like Ice Cream

The Scoop on Helping the Next Generation
Fall in Love with God's Word

Keith Ferrin

TYMK

Copyright © Keith Ferrin, 2011
Published by That You May Know Ministries
Book design: Brian Gage – www.pipetabor.com
Cover photo: Psd Photography – www.iStockphoto.com
Back kids photo: Monkey Business Photos – www.iStockphoto.com
Back cover family photo: Bruce Johnson – Rowland Studio, Seattle, WA

All Scripture quotations, unless otherwise indicated,
are taken from the Holy Bible, New International Version®, NIV®.
Copyright ©1973, 1978, 1984 by Biblica, Inc.™
Used by permission of Zondervan.
All rights reserved worldwide. www.zondervan.com

For information or to schedule author appearances:
That You May Know Ministries
PO Box 276
Kirkland, WA 98083
(425) 739-6070
www.thatyoumayknow.com
info@thatyoumayknow.com

ISBN: 978-0-9740023-1-6

Printed in the United States of America
by Applied Digital Imaging
Bellingham, Washington

*This book is dedicated to
Sarah, Caleb, and Hannah.
May you fall in love with
the Word and its Author…
just as naturally and
deeply as you fell in love
with ice cream.*

I love you.

Dad

Table of Contents

Acknowledgements

To say this book was a group effort would be a massive understatement. To thank everyone who contributed a story, idea, or resource that ended up on these pages would take more ink than the content itself.

There is the mother in Minnesota and the father in Oregon. There is the Sunday school teacher in England, the children's pastor in Missouri, and the youth pastor in Washington. Then there are the many emails and the countless conversations after presentations and workshops I have done in the last 15 years. To all of you who have helped shape not only the content of this book, but my own love for God's Word—thank you.

Kelly Humphreys—You helped edit and shape the words I wrote into something more accessible by those who hold this book. You even reminded me of the need for one of the chapters. I am grateful.

Brian Gage—Well, you did it again. You heard my heartbeat for this project and then worked your design magic. I love seeing the way you make ideas turn into visual artistry.

Kari—You have walked with me on this journey of helping our children fall in love with God and His Word. You have put up with the crazy schedule of a traveling speaker and writer. You continue to make our home a place where God's Word is not only read and honored, but lived out every day. You are the reason that I am smiling on every flight home.

Sarah, Caleb, and Hannah—Watching you grow is the most joyful part of my life on earth. Every time I think I couldn't possibly love you more, I look at the three of you and my heart grows again. I am thankful for the life and laughter you bring into our home. I am thankful for all that you have taught me about the abundance of the Father's love and my daily need for His mercy. And I am thankful in advance for every bowl of ice cream we will share together.

Lord Jesus—You are the Beautiful, Mysterious, Living Word. Thank You for allowing me to join You in bringing Your Kingdom here on earth and the promise of living in Your presence in Your Kingdom to come.

What's with the title?

Ice cream. Just saying the words brings a smile to my face. Also tempts me to stop writing, head downstairs, and open my freezer.

Let's get one thing right out in the open: *I love ice cream.*

Always have. I don't remember a time when ice cream wasn't a regular staple in the Ferrin Family Freezer. As I write these words there are three or four different flavors in our freezer right now! This love affair with ice cream started earlier than I can remember.

Growing up, there were two events that happened nearly every day in our home. Dinner as a family at 6pm. A bowl of ice cream at 8pm. To this day, it feels a bit strange when I am in someone else's home and dessert is served immediately following the meal. My stomach needs a little down time. But come 8pm - bring it on.

It doesn't need to be anything fancy. Usually something with the words *coffee* or *espresso* somewhere in the title. Currently, our favorite is *Coffee Fudge Chunk.* Ahhhh...three beautiful words. If there's no coffee ice cream in the house, I'm perfectly happy with peach, strawberry, caramel swirl, or even a simple scoop of vanilla.

You can blame it on my dad. After all, he's had the same love for ice cream - including the daily "6pm dinner/8pm ice cream" schedule - since he was a kid. So...I guess you had better blame Granddad Ferrin. Rumor has it, the ice cream addiction started with him. And guess what? All three of my kids love it too. Another generation of Ferrins hopelessly - and happily - addicted to ice cream.

Not too long ago, I was driving down the street and the thought came into my mind: *Am I passing down my love for God's Word the same way I am passing down my love for ice cream?* I am not just talking about *Am I doing it?*, but *Am I doing it **in the same way?*** Just as easily. Just as naturally. Just as joyfully.

I never sat my kids down and said, *Kids, here is what your mother and I love about ice cream. It's tasty. It's creamy. It's cool and smooth. It comes in so many delicious flavors.*

No. Not even close. I just ate it. Regularly. They saw me love it. I served it to them. Sometimes plain. Sometimes on a cone. Sometimes in a bowl with toppings. Sometimes simple. Sometimes really creative. And now they love it.

Take a look at the words of Asaph in Psalm 78:1-7:

> O my people, hear my teaching;
>   listen to the words of my mouth.
> I will open my mouth in parables,
>   I will utter hidden things, things from of old –
> what we have heard and known,
>   what our fathers have told us.
>
> We will not hide them from their children;
>   we will tell the next generation
>   the praiseworthy deeds of the LORD,
>   his power, and the wonders he has done.
>
> He decreed statutes for Jacob
>   and established the law in Israel,
>   which he commanded our forefathers
>   to teach their children,
>
> so the next generation would know them,
>   even the children yet to be born,
>   and they in turn would tell their children.
>
> Then they would put their trust in God
>   and would not forget his deeds
>   but would keep his commands.

These verses are the essence of this book. I long for my kids to know the God who formed them, loves them, and rejoices over them. Not just intellectually know Him, but *relationally* know Him. I don't think that can be done without them also developing a love for God's Word.

I want my love for God's Word to be passed on to them as it was passed on to me. And I long for that love to be passed on to their kids... *even the children yet to be born, and they in turn would tell their children. Then they would put their trust in God.*

I want that love to be generational. Just like ice cream.

Principle One:

Love it yourself.

"*Setting an example is not the main means of influencing another, it is the only means.*"

—Albert Einstein

"*Preach the Gospel at all times. If necessary, use words.*"

—Francis of Assisi

Like Ice Cream

Have you ever done anything in front of the ever-watchful eyes of a child and then immediately wished you could take it back? Well, I have enough material for a book entitled *Parenting Moments I'm Not Proud Of*.

One story that would definitely make the cut started out innocently enough. We were hanging out in the living room when my then five-year-old son walked past me. Without even thinking about it, I gave his very loose-fitting shorts a little tug and they quickly dropped to his knees. He yelped out a surprised "Hey!" His older sister laughed, Kari rolled her eyes, Caleb then proceeded to jump on me, and mayhem ensued.

It took very little time for me to learn once again about the power of example. Several times over the next couple days, Caleb not only tried to do the same thing to me (unsuccessfully), but also to his seven-year-old sister (successfully). The yelps that followed weren't so pleasant and the laughter was nonexistent. And of course, the request – then command – of his mother to cut it out was met with the dreaded "but Daddy did it to me" rebuttal. Heavy sigh.

Whether it has to do with what we do, what we say, or even our attitudes in general, any parent – or anyone who has ever worked with kids for that matter – can tell you that kids do what they *see*, not what they are told. And God knows that better than anyone. I think that is why in Deuteronomy 6, immediately after telling us to love God with everything we've got, we find these words:

> **These commandments that I give you today are to be upon your hearts.** *Impress them on your children. Talk about them, when you sit at home and when you walk along the road, when you lie down and when you get up. Tie them as symbols on your hands and bind them on your foreheads. Write them on the doorframes of your houses and on your gates.* (Deut 6:6-9, emphasis added)

When laying out all of the "how-tos" of loving God with all our heart, soul, and strength, notice where God begins. Before telling the Israelites to impress the word on their children, He reminded them that this love for God and His Word needed to start with *them*. The same is true today. It needs to start with us.

Make an honest assessment.

How are you doing when it comes to loving God and His Word? If your mind went immediately toward guilt for how inconsistent you are in your Bible reading - or pride for how frequently you read - then let me remind you of the analogy driving this whole book: ice cream. I don't love ice cream because I force myself to eat it. I eat it because I already love it - whether I am *currently eating it or not!*

> I don't love ice cream because I force myself to eat it. I eat it because I already love it!

A more honest way to assess how you are doing may be to ask some of these questions:

- Do I actually enjoy the Bible when I read it? Do I ever talk about the Bible or God with anyone?
- Do I ever find myself in the car with the radio off, because I just need some time to talk - or listen! - to God?
- Do I ever think about what God's opinion is of what I am doing, the language I use, the media I put before my eyes and into my ears, or the conversations I engage in?
- Do I ever look at God's creation and utter a heartfelt, awe-filled "Thank You" under my breath?
- How would I answer the question *What have you and God done for fun lately?*[1]
- Are there parts of my day - or elements of my life - that are "off limits" to God?

Like Ice Cream

When it comes to assessing our relationship with God, we all too often boil it down to a list of religious activities that we somehow think will "make God happy." Twenty minutes of Bible reading – check. Weekly church attendance – check. Ten minutes of prayer – check. God must be happy, right? Well...maybe. Maybe not. What other relationships would you boil down to a To Do List? None, I hope!

Now...are there things we should and shouldn't do? Sure. Are there activities that will foster or hinder our relationship with God? Absolutely. But the "doing of the thing" is not the relationship itself. This idea is so central to everything we are going to explore in this book that it warrants repeating: The "doing of the thing" is *not* the relationship itself. Pause for a moment and let that sink in.

It is also not the scope of this chapter to lay out a full plan for how to deepen your relationship with God. In fact, I think many of the *activities* I just mentioned (Bible reading, church attendance, prayer, etc.) should be included in this process. However, the *purpose* we have as we approach these activities is essential. The purpose is relationship. The purpose is knowing God, not just knowing about Him. The purpose is loving God, not just appeasing Him (or our false sense of what we think would appease Him).

When it comes to the Bible specifically – which is, after all, the primary focus of this book – I know that I spent the first two decades I was a Christian not really *liking* the Bible very much. Sure, I believed it was true. But I can't say I loved reading it. My first book, *Falling in Love with God's Word: Discovering What God Always Intended Bible Study To Be*, tells of my journey toward loving God's Word. It also lays out my approach to studying the Bible *relationally*, rather than *informationally*. If you haven't read that book, it might be a good place to start.

An even better idea is to take note of the people you know who genuinely enjoy the Bible. Ask them how they approach the Bible. Listen to them tell of their journey toward loving God and His Word. You will certainly learn some practical ideas, as well as be encouraged to take the next step on your own journey.

So, it starts with an honest assessment. And this may be obvious (but still needs to be said): our personal journey toward loving God's Word is a journey without end. This leads me right into what we do after we have made our honest assessment.

Let them see our journey.

An interesting thing has happened in the Ferrin Household this last year. I made one little change that has had great impact on family discussions about the Bible. I moved. All the way from my office to the living room couch.

Until this year, I had always had my early morning time in my office. Comfy chair. Quiet room. The laptop is right there if I want to look something up. This year, I decided to move downstairs. Now, I grab my Bible – and occasionally my laptop – and plop down on the couch. Then I read until my first child wakes up and sleepily meanders down the stairs.

The next few minutes usually involves one of them crawling up onto my lap, pulling the blanket over us both, and then just sitting silently or chatting for a while. I am not going to say that every morning we have an amazing, life-changing, music-playing, angels-singing spiritual conversation. Sometimes we just sit. Sometimes we watch the hummingbirds eating breakfast at our back porch feeder. And sometimes one of my kids will say "Dad, what were you reading about today?" Other times I will say "Hey, you wouldn't believe the story I just read in the Bible!" And off we'll go...

Just as importantly, there will be times when we are walking home from school, driving down the road, or eating a snack (ahem...ice cream), when one of them will mention my "Bible time" in the mornings. They might be asking a question about it. Typically they are just mentioning it as part of another conversation. Either way, the lesson they are learning is *Daddy likes to read his Bible.* They know it is important to me. They know it is a regular part of my daily life. They *see* it.

Ahhhh...seeing it. This has enormous impact on kids. It is also something that doesn't happen nearly enough. Even if we are in the Word regularly, our kids may only see us with our Bibles on Sundays.

Do our kids know what we are reading? Do we ever talk about it with them? Do they see us in the Word? If you are a youth pastor, do you ever talk with your students about something you have been reading or studying (other than when it pertains to the "lesson" for the week)?

Like Ice Cream

The next generation has got to see our journey. The lessons we are learning. The struggles we are having. The stories we are enjoying. The habits we are creating. All of it. If there is one thing I have learned about the next generation is that they can sniff out authenticity – and inauthenticity – a mile away. When they see the Bible as something that is real, relevant, and enjoyable to us, they will be a lot more likely to join us on that journey.

> The next generation has got to see our journey. The lessons we are learning. The struggles we are having. The stories we are enjoying. The habits we are creating. All of it.

---

[1] When I was a youth pastor, my lead pastor – Doug Olson – would frequently use this question when leading small groups of men. The first time he asked it, I raised a curious eyebrow. The more I thought about it, the more perfect this question sounded when trying to assess if I was actually in a relationship with God – or just going through the motions. Thanks Doug.

Your own ideas for putting Principle One into practice...

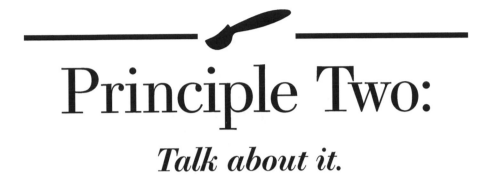

Principle Two:

Talk about it.

"There is no such thing as a worthless conversation, provided you know what to listen for."

—James Nathan Miller

Like Ice Cream

People talk all the time, about everything. Sports. Weather. School. Activities. Technology. Friends. Movies. Music. You name it – we talk about it. When I think about the different hobbies, foods, or sports teams that I love, I can typically trace it back to conversations I had with someone who loved that hobby, food, or sports team before I did. Simply put: *Whatever we talk about we become more interested in.*

Understanding this principle, let's return to Deuteronomy 6:

> *These commandments that I give you today are to be upon your hearts. Impress them on your children.* **Talk about them, when you sit at home and when you walk along the road, when you lie down and when you get up.** *Tie them as symbols on your hands and bind them on your foreheads. Write them on the doorframes of your houses and on your gates.* (Deut 6:6-9, emphasis added)

As we saw in the previous chapter, God reminds us that the starting point for helping the next generation fall in love with His Word is us. He then makes the statement "Impress them on your children." The rest of the paragraph – and the remainder of this book – looks at how to do that.

Immediately after saying, "Impress them on your children," the next sentence challenges us to talk about God's Word. And just to make sure we don't say, "We talk about the Bible at church, youth group, and Sunday school, so we've got that one covered," God makes it clear that talking about God's Word is an all-the-time-and-everywhere habit we need to develop.

- When you sit at home. (Hmmm....Doesn't sound like just church, youth group, and Sunday school.)
- When you walk along the road. (You mean out in the real world?!).

Talk about it.

- When you get up. (How do you start the day with your kids?)
- When you lie down. (What does your last conversation of the day with your kids look like?)

We are going to explore the second one ("...*when you walk along the road...*") in the next chapter, but the first, third, and fourth all happen in the home.[1] What are the conversations in your home like? How often are there *intentional* conversations about God and His Word in your home?

> There are many times during my daily reading where I'll see something exciting and I'll re-read the passage to my son. Sometimes I'll be goofy and make the story fun and sometimes I'll be very serious depending on the story and make it like a play as I read in different voices for different characters. He loves that! —Brad (father)

When you sit at home...

I don't know about you, but with traveling, writing, Kari's teaching, school work, play dates, Sarah's soccer, Caleb's soccer, and Hannah's... well...two-year-old-ness, I can't say there is a lot of time that I would describe as "when you sit at home." That said, our busy schedule does not excuse Kari and me from obeying God's call on us as parents. Rob Rienow talks about the same thing in his terrific book, *Visionary Parenting*:

As I wrestled with this simple instruction from God to talk about His Word with my family at home, I told Him in prayer that, because of my schedule, I did not have time for that! God was far more gracious with me than I deserved. I felt God respond to that moronic prayer with a firm but gentle message. "Rob, if your schedule is preventing you from sitting at home and talking about Me with your family, then the schedule you have chosen is causing you to sin." I was being disobedient to the very first action point and responsibility that I had as a parent. Ouch![2]

Like Ice Cream

We are certainly far from perfect examples of this, but we are striving to weave spiritual conversations into the everyday mayhem of the Ferrin Family Home. Sometimes it is simply a quick mention of our gratefulness to God for giving us a warm house on a cold, winter night. Other times it is a much longer conversation about our attitudes, kindness, compassion, or generosity (just to name a few). Frequently, it is woven into those teachable moments when siblings are pushing the buttons only they know how to push!

> **One thing we have learned is that the more we talk about the lessons in Scripture, the more our kids bring it up.**

One thing we have learned is that the more we talk about the lessons in Scripture, the more *our kids bring it up.* This ends up leading to more conversations. And when they start the conversation, they are infinitely more apt to listen and not just see it as *Daddy and Mommy teaching us another lesson.*

Here is one of the more humorous times this happened. The conversation went something like this:

Sarah: *Ouch! Daaaaaaddddddy....Caleb hit me!*
Me: *Caleb. Did you hit your sister?*
Caleb: *Yes.*
Me: *Why did you hit her?*
Caleb: *Well, the Bible says "Do to others as you would have them do to you." She hit me first, so I thought she wanted me to.*
Me: *Caleb, that's not exactly what that means.*
(Trying not to chuckle at the terrific logic of it all.)

And off we went into a conversation about how *you* want to be treated, not just mirroring the actions of other people. But the encouraging thing for me was that Caleb would even *think* about what the Bible has to say. Somewhere along the line, we had talked about that. And it stuck.

When you get up...

Let me say right up front – mornings are tough. There is simply not much time between when the kids wake up and when we head out the door to school. In our home, we have not gotten the routine down yet, but we are working on it.

I received one email from someone with nine-year-old twins who has been reading the Bible to her kids every morning since they came home from the hospital. We are not there yet. But we are trying. It is too important *not* to try.

So frequently, what happens in the morning sets the tone for the day. A harsh conversation, bad traffic, or oversleeping can make us feel "off" for hours and hours. However, the opposite is also true. Having a good conversation, a delicious cup of coffee, or some quiet time to think and pray can certainly help me feel "on" throughout the day. The same is also true with our kids.

A few practical questions to help us think about how we might live this out in the mornings:

- What if we made it a point to read one or two encouraging verses from the Bible as our kids chomped down their bowls of cereal?
- What if we established a "verse for the day" or "verse for the week" routine where the whole family was internalizing and discussing the same verse?
- How would our kids handle their relationships with their friends differently if they were reminded each morning of who they are in Christ? Reminded that they are valuable, cherished, and of immeasurable worth in your eyes – and in the eyes of the One who created them, died for them, and lives with them.
- What if we read a short piece from one of the many good family devotional books that are out there?[3]
- What if we spent even a few minutes asking our kids how we could be praying for them that day? Or better yet... *actually praying* with our kids before they leave for school, soccer, work, etc.?

My guess is that it would not only mean a whole lot to our kids, but it would go a long way toward putting *us* in the right frame of mind to tackle the day!

When you lie down...

There is just something about night time. All throughout my life, I can look back to so many late-night conversations that had a lot of meaning. Sometimes those conversations were with my parents as they sat on my bed and we "processed" the day. But not always. Conversations with my mom frequently happened as I sat at the kitchen counter and she baked something or prepared for the next day.

Many times when I was in high school, I would walk into my dad's office before heading to bed and plop down into the chair near his desk. One of us would ask a question or start a story. The next thing we knew it was an hour later and off I would head to bed.

In college, late at night was when all of us know-it-all 20-year-olds solved every major world problem. We talked about faith. We talked about life. We talked about sports. We talked about the fairer gender. And no kidding, if these conversations weren't in the dorm over pizza, we were at the on-campus hangout (called The Cave) eating ice cream!

The importance of the late-night conversations continued when I became a youth pastor. You want to get teenagers to talk to you? Any youth pastor will tell you that all it takes is to provide pizza or ice cream sundaes *starting* at 10pm...or later! I guarantee you that they will talk longer than you can keep your eyes open.

And now that we have little ones in the house, we continue to see the specialness of the hour before bed. Before going on, let me be up front about the fact that more often than I would like to admit, the hour before bed is very frustrating. All three of our kids have mastered the art of The Bedtime Stall. You know what I am talking about. You have seen it. You have experienced the endless stream of *I'm thirsty. I have to go the bathroom. I'm not tired. Just one more book...pleeeeeeease?*

That said, I still believe that the minutes before we turn off their lights hold a special opportunity for us to connect with our kids. Our kids are much more cuddly at bedtime than any other time. They want to be near us. They want us to read to them.

The temptation – since I am frequently tired and just want to go sit down on the couch – is to read a book as quickly as I can, say a 10-second prayer, and head out of the room. But in an occasional moment of clarity and wisdom, I will ask them a question, read them a Bible story, or just listen to them tell me about their day. I can't remember a single time I regretted spending the extra time.

Recently, I have started having the last thing I read to them be one of the Psalms. So many of the Psalms are honest conversations - for good and for bad - which the psalmist had with God. Just last night I read Psalm 138 to the kids, which ends with the following words:

> The Lord will fulfill His purpose
>   for me;
> Your love, O Lord, endures
>   forever –
> do not abandon the works of
>   Your hands.

Then I simply said, "As you go to bed tonight, just remember that everything God wants you to do and be, He will make sure it happens. God is with you and loves you...forever."

We didn't have an earth-shaking spiritual conversation after I read. In fact, the kids didn't say anything. But that was okay. They heard their father sharing the words - and ideas - of Scripture in a way that was encouraging, affirming, and relational. If our kids are going to grow up believing that the Bible - and more importantly, the Author! - is relational, then they need to see us talking about it with them relationally.

> People know that I am in love with my wife because I'm always referring to her in conversation. When we are in love we want to talk about the one we love.
> —Mike

If the Bible is just something we talk about when it is time to "study" it, then it will never be relational to them. They will never love it. But if we have conversations about God's Word in the morning, at night, and in the normal ebb and flow of our day, they will come to know the Bible as something relevant, real, and enjoyable.

[1] If you are a youth pastor or children's pastor, you might want to share the content of this chapter with the parents of your students.

[2] Rob Rienow, *Visionary Parenting*, (Randall House, 2009), pg 11.

[3] See Appendix 2 for some resources to get you started.

Your own ideas for putting Principle Two into practice...

Principle Three:

Make it real.

"*A good example is far better than a good precept.*"
—Dwight L. Moody

"*Our faith has to connect with the world we live in.*"
—Shane Claiborne

Like Ice Cream

I t started several years ago. We would be driving down the street and hear a siren or see an ambulance. Usually it was Kari who would say, "Hey guys. Let's pray for the people that the ambulance is on their way to help." We would pray as we drove – for the record, my eyes were always open! – and then we would continue on our way.

These days, before Kari and I even *hear* the siren, one of our kids will say, "Hear that? We need to pray." This one application of the Apostle Paul's exhortation to *"pray continually"* (I Thess. 5:17) has now become something that our kids do consistently – without our prodding. They have connected the *words* of Scripture with the *reality* of everyday life.

I could not agree more with Shane Claiborne's quote at the beginning of this chapter. *Our faith has to connect with the world we live in.* Let's see where this shows up in the Deuteronomy 6 passage we have been looking at:

> *These commandments that I give you today are to be upon your hearts. Impress them on your children. Talk about them, when you sit at home and **when you walk along the road**, when you lie down and when you get up. Tie them as symbols on your hands and bind them on your foreheads. Write them on the doorframes of your houses and on your gates.* (Deut. 6:6-9, emphasis added)

> If we want the next generation to fall in love with God's Word we have no choice but to help them see the Bible's relevance when they are at school, with their friends, on the soccer field, or on their computers.

Sitting at home...lying down...getting up. These all happen at home. But *walking along the road?* That covers everything else. Talking about the

Make it real.

Bible – and our entire life of faith for that matter – can't be compartmentalized to our own homes and Sunday mornings. If we want the next generation to fall in love with God's Word we have no choice but to help them see the Bible's relevance when they are at school, with their friends, on the soccer field, or on their computers.

Without a connection to real life, faith and the Bible will end up being discarded as things that, quite simply, don't matter. That might sound harsh, but the truth is this: The next generation will not waste time on things that don't make a difference to them. Doing or believing something because you are *supposed to*, or because your parents did it or believed it, is not a good enough reason.

One of our primary jobs in raising and positively influencing the next generation is to help them see and experience that connection. Can that happen in the home, at youth group, and during Sunday school? I should hope so! But if those three are the only places they are connecting to God and His Word, is that enough for them to make a lifelong commitment? Not a chance.

When I see *"when you walk along the road"* thrown in the mix, I can only come to the conclusion that God sees the connection between His Word and everyday life as essential – not just a nice add-on.

So how do we do it? During my time as a youth pastor – and now as a parent – I have learned that the most important ingredient for making that connection is to *pay attention*. That might sound simple enough, but the more that we intentionally look for times when the stories, lessons, truths, and ideas that we have read in the Bible connect to what we see in everyday life, the more likely we are to bring them up conversationally. And that is huge.

The next generation loves conversation. They are not so fond of getting "taught" something. If *they* ask the question – teach your heart out. If *you* are bringing it up, make it a conversation. There are obviously an infinite number of possibilities, but here are few ideas to get you started:

- Talk about what God's Word says about compassion and poverty while driving to and from serving dinner at your local shelter.
- Discuss money and generosity as you are walking through the store.

- Talk through Genesis 1 while taking a hike or visiting the zoo.
- Spend the drive/walk to school discussing what is coming up in their day – and then pray about it!
- Talk about God's vision for purity while shopping for a prom dress. (And don't leave out God's vision and desire for us to celebrate and have a blast!)
- Insert 3,000,000 of your own ideas here!

A story from our family

This power of weaving the truths of Scripture into everyday life became abundantly clear to our family because of a man named Clayton Samuel. Kari and the kids first met Clayton Samuel (they always call him by both names) one day while heading to the zoo. He was on one of the corners holding a sign asking for food. One of the kids asked Kari what the sign said and when she told them, they decided to give him some food from their snack bag.

The next time they were headed that way, they decided to actually *bring something* in case they saw him. There he was. This time they gave him the food, but they also asked him his name and how they could pray for him. Over the next year, this scene played out several times. During one of their 20-second chats, Clayton Samuel mentioned that he knew and loved Jesus too. Our kids' faces beamed.

These chats with Clayton Samuel led to many conversations about homelessness. What causes it? What does the Bible say our responsibility is as followers of Jesus? How can we help? One day, out of the blue, Caleb enthusiastically said, "We have extra room in our house. What if everyone who has extra room in their houses let someone who is homeless stay there? There would be no more homeless people!" More conversations...

> For too many children, Bible reading is either all adventure or all "have to." To really get them to fall in love with God's Word, they have to recognize how personal and relevant it really is. —Nicole (mother)

Make it real.

During one trip they noticed that Clayton Samuel wasn't on "his corner." The next time, someone else was there. Hoping that this person knew Clayton Samuel, they asked where he was. "He passed away three weeks ago" was the response. Silence. Then Sarah quietly asked, "So, he's with Jesus now? And he's not homeless?" Kari said, "Yes. You're right. Clayton Samuel has a home now. Forever." More conversations...

It has been almost a year since Clayton Samuel went home. Just last week, we went to the zoo. On the way home, we drove by Clayton Samuel's corner. One of our kids mentioned Clayton Samuel. He's a person to them. Not a "homeless" person. Just a real, live person. Oh... and they can't wait to see him again someday. To think it all started with a conversation in the car on the way to the zoo.

Your own ideas for putting Principle Three into practice…

Principle Four:

Remind them of who it says they are.

"I am convinced that so many of the damaging choices we've made in our lives are because of one fundamental amnesia issue. We forget who we really are."

—Ron Hutchcraft

"There is no perception-vs.-reality. Perception is reality."

Anonymous

Like Ice Cream

As we continue our five-chapter journey through Deuteronomy 6, the last two phrases might seem a bit odd. Let's take a look:

> *These commandments that I give you today are to be upon your hearts. Impress them on your children. Talk about them, when you sit at home and when you walk along the road, when you lie down and when you get up.* **Tie them as symbols on your hands and bind them on your foreheads.** *Write them on the doorframes of your houses and on your gates.* (Deut. 6:6-9, emphasis added)

Symbols on your hands? Binding them on your foreheads? Writing them on your doorframes and gates? Really? Is this a call to get tattoos and paint our houses? I don't think so. (Though some teenagers I know will probably try to use these verses when having the can-I-get-a-tattoo conversation.) We will look at just the *"hands and foreheads"* part in this chapter and explore the *"houses and gates"* part in the next.

Now, there is certainly historical context for the idea that some Scriptures were deemed so valuable that devout people would carry them with them all the time. (This passage from Deuteronomy 6 is actually one of those Scriptures!) They would literally tie them around their forearms and put them in small boxes (called phylacteries) that would be fastened around their foreheads. People could see the Scriptures wrapped around your hands and on your foreheads and know immediately whether you were a Jew or not. It was an *identity* issue.

This started making a lot more sense to me in the spring of 1998. I was the assistant coach of a high school boys' soccer team. This particular day was Picture Day. The photographer was getting more frustrated by the minute. Why? Because right before snapping the picture several of the players would flash gang signs. They knew that the symbols they made with their hands helped mark their identities. Not only that, but this was in the 90's when different gangs would tie red or blue bandanas around their heads to identify which gang they ran with. What they did with their hands and what they wore on their foreheads marked their identity.

Group identity is certainly important to all of us – including the next generation. We will talk more about that in the next chapter. But your hands and your foreheads are yours – and yours alone. Young, old, rich, poor, male, female doesn't matter. Your identity – what you believe to be true about yourself – is vital to the decisions you make every day.

> # Think of one young person you know. What does she believe about herself?

What are the "identity" messages that the next generation is hearing? More specifically: Think of one young person you know. What does she believe about herself? Who does he think he is? What are you telling her about her identity in Christ? Does he know – truly *know* – that he is a beloved child of the King of all creation? Has she heard that the One who made her calls her *beautiful*...and means it? Are you telling him that he is forgiven – completely?

I could spend pages and pages writing about identity. I think this is a massive issue for the next generation – and for all of us! But rather than just sharing my theories about the next generation, let's spend the remainder of this chapter looking at what the Bible says about our identity in Christ.

First, slowly and prayerfully read through this list. Afterward, I will share some ideas of how you can use it.

These next several minutes are the only time during your reading of this book that I want you to *not* think about the next generation. Don't think of anyone else. For right now, this list is for you...

- *You are a child of God. (I John 3:1)*
- *You may participate in the divine nature. (I Peter 1:4)*
- *You have a mighty God who is for you...not against you. (Romans 8:31)*
- *You have been crucified with Christ and you no longer live, but Christ lives in you. (Galatians 2:20)*

Like Ice Cream

- *You have access to the throne of God – where you can receive mercy and find grace.* (Hebrews 4:16)
- *You have been raised with Christ and seated with Him in the heavenly realm.* (Ephesians 1:6)
- *You are part of God's family.* (Hebrews 2:11)
- *You have been blessed with every spiritual blessing in Christ.* (Ephesians 1:3)
- *You have everything you need for life and godliness.* (I Peter 1:3)
- *You have been bought with a price.* (I Corinthians 6:20)
- *You were called to be free.* (Galatians 5:13)
- *You have been ransomed by the Son of God.* (Matthew 20:28)
- *You are not condemned.* (Romans 8:1)
- *You have been forgiven.* (Acts 10:43)
- *You have become the righteousness of God.* (II Corinthians 5:21)
- *You are God's workmanship...His poem...His masterpiece.* (Ephesians 2:10)
- *You have been set free from the law of sin.* (Romans 8:2)
- *You have been made alive with Christ.* (Ephesians 2:5)
- *You have been given the authority of Christ.* (Luke 10:19)
- *You have been fearfully and wonderfully made.* (Psalm 139:14)
- *You are dead to sin and alive to God.* (Romans 6:11)
- *You were chosen by God before the creation of the world.* (Ephesians 1:4)
- *You are destined for glorious freedom.* (Romans 8:21)
- *You are a citizen of Heaven.* (Philippians 3:20)
- *You are more than a conqueror through Him who loved you.* (Romans 8:37)
- *You have been baptized with Christ and are now clothed with Christ.* (Galatians 3:27)
- *You have been brought from death to life.* (Romans 6:13)
- *You have been given the Holy Spirit to guide you into all truth.* (John 16:13)
- *You have been redeemed and have the full rights of sons.* (Galatians 4:5)
- *You are protected by the powerful name of Jesus.* (John 17:11)
- *You have the power of the Holy Spirit.* (Acts 1:8)

Remind them of who it says they are.

- You have a High Priest who is able to sympathize with your weaknesses. (Hebrews 4:13)
- You have the Holy Spirit interceding for you right now. (Romans 8:26)
- Your Lord is near. (Philippians 4:5)
- You are known. (Psalm 139:1)
- You cannot be separated from the love of God that is in Christ Jesus. (Romans 8:38-39)
- You are a work in progress – and you will be completed. (Philippians 1:6)
- You were loved by Jesus before you loved Him. (I John 4:19)
- You are not alone. (Deuteronomy 31:6)
- You have the full armor of God...

  ...the belt of truth

  ...the breastplate of righteousness

  ...the shoes of the gospel of peace

  ...the shield of faith

  ...the helmet of salvation

  ...the sword of the Spirit – the Word of God. (Ephesians 6:13-17)
- You have God's angels sent to serve you. (Hebrews 1:14)
- Your needs will be met according to God's glorious riches in Christ Jesus. (Philippians 4:19)
- You have a High Priest who always lives to intercede for you. (Hebrews 7:25)
- You have a God who has gone before you. (Psalm 59:10)
- You have a God who hears you. (I John 5:14)
- You cannot be snatched from God's hand. (John 10:28-29)
- God is for you. (Psalm 56:9)
- You are Jesus' joy. (Hebrews 12:2)
- You are loved. (John 3:16)

What if you actually believed what you just read? What if your identity were shaped by these truths? Now...what if the child or student you were thinking of earlier in this chapter actually grew up having these truths shape his or her identity from this day forward? Powerful doesn't begin to describe it.

Like Ice Cream

A few ideas to get you started:

- Read this list at least once a week.
- Read and discuss one truth on this list each morning over breakfast.
- Read and discuss one truth on this list right before bedtime so your child is thinking these thoughts after you leave the room.
- Have your youth group discuss one – or a few – of these truths each week for several weeks. It could be a *"Who are you... really?"* series.
- Have your Sunday school classes write, dramatize, draw, or discuss what these would look like "lived out."
- Put each of these truths on a card that you stick to your child's bathroom mirror each morning.
- Discuss one of these truths on the walk/drive to school, soccer practice, the store, or your next family vacation.

Your own ideas for putting Principle Four into practice...

Principle Five:

Surround them with people who love it.

"The Christian faith requires community. I cannot follow Jesus alone any more than I can get married alone."

—Timothy Paul Jones

"Children have never been very good at listening to their elders, but they have never failed to imitate them."

—James Arthur Baldwin

He was holding a cucumber. During a sermon. Can't say I had ever seen that before. I was a youth pastor and our lead pastor paused in the middle of his sermon, reached over, and grabbed a cucumber. What he said next has stuck in my head for almost 20 years. "The only thing that is going to make this cucumber a sweet pickle instead of a dill pickle is what I soak it in."[1]

I can't read the last sentence of this paragraph from Deuteronomy 6 without having those words play in my head. Let's read it one more time:

> *These commandments that I give you today are to be upon your hearts. Impress them on your children. Talk about them, when you sit at home and when you walk along the road, when you lie down and when you get up. Tie them as symbols on your hands and bind them on your foreheads.* **Write them on the doorframes of your houses and on your gates.** (Deut. 6:6-9, emphasis added)

In the last chapter we talked about how your hands and foreheads are yours – and yours alone. On the other hand, when I think of the doorframe of a house, or a gate, the image in my head is of an intimate group of people. A family. A club. A church.

> Bottom line: Are our kids soaking in relationships shaped and guided by the **Word** or the **world**?

Who are the people that your son, daughter, or student are "soaking" in? Are they helping you *write God's Word* on the doorframes and gates where your kids live, play, and hang out? As a youth pastor, are you helping create a youth group where God's Word is *lived out* – not just *taught*? Are we monitoring – and investing in – the friends that our kids spend hours and hours with, process life with (with less and less input from us as they get older), and are influenced by? Bottom line: Are our kids soaking in relationships shaped and guided by the *Word* or the *world?*

There are so many places where this is important. Making sure that our homes are places where our kids are soaking in the Word is an obvious focus of much of this book. But as you know, the older kids get, the less time they spend at home. School. Sports. Band. Friends. Work. The list goes on...

Friends

As a parent, one of the many challenges I see is that so many of those away-from-home places are situations where I don't control the influences and messages my children are hearing. However, when I *can* have an influence – I do!

Later today I will be volunteering in my son's classroom. I won't be reading the Bible to Caleb and his classmates, but I will be treating them with as much kindness and love as I can. Not only that, but I will be *paying attention* to what is happening in the classroom. This will provide the opportunity for me to have a conversation with Caleb later about the good and bad messages we both heard.

With both Caleb and Sarah, I have either coached or help coach as many teams as my schedule will allow. T-ball? Yep. Softball? Did that too. Soccer? Absolutely. Gymnastics? Ok...gotta draw the line somewhere. For some of these teams I was an assistant who helped occasionally at practice or kept score during the game. For Sarah's softball team I even earned the weekly title of "Dugout Mom." (You can stop giggling now.)

Last week, I just wrapped up my first season of being the head coach of Sarah's soccer team. Each week at practice and the games, I tried to teach the girls about respect, being a team, noticing the good in someone else's actions and attitudes, and being proud of hard work. Without quoting Bible verses, I was certainly teaching Bible *principles.* How cool it was when, at the end-of-the-year pizza party, one of the dads even came up to me and thanked me for continually reinforcing these messages!

With Sarah and Caleb I actually *did* bring specific Scriptures into the conversation. Most recently it was this Proverb:

Let another praise you, and not your own mouth; someone else, and not your own lips. Proverbs 27:2

We talked about the importance of humility – as well as praising others. The Bible was brought into everyday life. (Remember Principle Three?)

Church

While we should always keep an eye out for ways to influence the environments our kids are in, there are two more specific areas I would like to explore in this chapter. The first is church. Is church the primary discipleship and Bible-learning, Bible-loving environment for the next generation? Not at all. That's the job of the home.[2] That said, the church is a vital part of the equation.

Kari and I are blessed to be part of a church community where Jesus is worshipped, the next generation is celebrated and valued, and the Bible is not just taught – but loved. The example of Jesus valuing children is lived out throughout the church. One of our drummers started playing when he was about 12 (and he is now in his mid-20's). The kids' Christmas drama is always one of the best-attended and most-enjoyed events of the year. And Sunday school is a place where our kids have a blast and learn lots about the Bible. Frequently, I will be reading or telling my kids a Bible story and one of them will add to it – or tell me that I have missed something. Come to find out, they had already learned the story at church.

I love that my kids are growing up with teachers who love them, model Jesus to them, and tie it all back to God's Word. These other adults – and some older high schoolers – are writing God's Word on the doorframes and gates of our church. And our kids are reaping the benefits.

Small Group

Speaking of other adults, this leads me to the last area I want to cover in this chapter: the small group. Your church may call them home groups, life groups, care groups, home Bible studies, or something way more creative, but the concept is still the same. Get a handful of couples or families together and eat, study, pray, worship, cry, laugh, and celebrate – together.

We currently have two small groups – each meeting every other week. One has been meeting a little over a year. The hope is to invite new families and eventually split into two, invite new families, split into two, and so on.

However, our other small group is made up of five families that have been "doing life" together for the better part of a decade. The oldest child in this group is 15 as of this writing. When we started meeting together he was six. There are 12 children in our small group (17 if you count the husbands). None of them can ever remember a time in their lives when "small group" wasn't a regular part of the family schedule!

These 12 children have seen us laughing together, praying for each other, watching video series, and studying the Bible together. Sometimes the kids are involved in the discussion. Sometimes they are just having a good time upstairs. But even then, they are seeing the adults in their lives caring for each other, and making God's Word a priority (see Principle Nine).

This has spilled over into so many areas other than just the two-hour, every-other-week small group. We have shown up at the school plays, band concerts, and sporting events of each other's kids. Do you know how powerful it is for a teenager to have an adult who doesn't "have to" love them show up at one of their games or events?

> Do you know how powerful it is for a teenager to have an adult who doesn't "have to" love them show up at one of their games or events?

Every youth pastor reading this book knows it full well. When you show students you value them, you gain trust. When you have trust, you have an opportunity for influence. Teaching students the Bible without having their trust and without having them feel valued will lead nowhere. Honestly, it will likely lead to a *negative* opinion about Jesus, the church, and other Christians. But when you model to them that they are valuable to you, and *then* you show them that the God of the Bible values them too – *that* is powerful.

I am convinced that helping the next generation fall in love with God's Word *must* be a community effort. The more that the next generation soaks in relationships – with peers and us older folks – that are "marked" by a love and longing for God and His Word, the more that love and longing will grow in them.

Like Ice Cream

---

[1]Thanks to Doug Olson who was my pastor and boss at Hope Covenant Church in Tacoma, WA for most of the '90s.

[2]If you are a youth pastor, then you know already that some of the students in your sphere of influence are getting no Biblical support, encouragement, or training at home. Your youth program – and you specifically – might very well be their primary discipleship center and Biblical role model. Some of the great memories I have of my days as a youth pastor were the times I saw a student get so excited about Jesus that her parents started coming to events, asking questions, and engaging in conversations with me and other members of our church community.

Your own ideas for putting Principle Five into practice...

Principle Six:

Pray about it.

"Don't let Satan rob you of the joy of praying for your kids – and of seeing God work in their lives."

—Jodie Berndt

"No one can come to me unless the Father who sent me draws him."

—Jesus (John 6:44)

I don't pray for my kids enough. There...I said it. I know I should. I certainly want them to grow up knowing and loving God and His Word. And I know the Word tells me that, through prayer, I have access to the very Throne Room of the Almighty. And yet, I don't pray for my kids nearly enough. How about you?

I am convinced that prayer is essential if the next generation is going to grow in their love and knowledge of the Word. This chapter is not going to explore all the different ways we can pray for our children. There are many tremendous books already written on that subject.[1] I simply want to lay out four *areas* where prayer is vital when it comes to the next generation falling in love with God's Word.

Pray for God to draw them.

In John 6, Jesus is talking to a pretty hostile crowd. Understandable, since He's talking about being the "bread of life," coming down from the Father, eating His flesh, and drinking His blood! In the middle of this conversation (verse 44) He says, *"No one can come to me unless the Father who sent me draws him."* Jesus must be pretty serious about this, because 21 verses later – as the crowd is getting increasingly hostile – He says again, *"This is why I told you that no one can come to me unless the Father has enabled him."*

Do we believe this? Do we really believe that the next generation *can't* come to Jesus unless the Father draws and enables them? More pointedly – Do we *pray* as if we believe it? As I mentioned a few paragraphs ago, my answer is sadly, "No." But I need to. And I am getting better.

If we really believed this, wouldn't we be on our knees, pleading with the Father to draw our children to Himself and enable them to come to Him? When it comes to praying for my kids, my life needs to reflect much more clearly what I say I believe in my head.

Pray for them to love God's Word.

Our kids are bombarded with messages about who they are (see

Pray about it.

Principle Five), what they *should* do, what they *should* have, and how they *should* live. As you well know, many of these messages are contrary to what Scripture tells us. How are they going to be able to discern the truth from the lie without a love and understanding of God's Word?

This might sound harsh, but it is not enough for them to believe the Bible is *true*. Without a *love* for God's Word they won't read it. They won't engage in conversations about it. They won't talk to their friends about it. And the messages – while true – will get lost in the noisy tidal wave of untrue messages.

> Without a love for God's Word they won't read it. They won't engage in conversations about it. They won't talk to their friends about it. And the messages – while true – will get lost in the noisy tidal wave of untrue messages.

We need to pray that the next generation will believe the Bible's veracity – and that they will like it! Pray that they will see the *life* in the Living Word of God. Pray that they will have engaging, fun, thoughtful conversations about what they read. Pray that their souls will resonate – and even rejoice! – when they hear the truths of Scripture. Pray that the Bible will be so true and so enjoyable that every false message will be so obviously false that they won't even be tempted to believe it.

Pray for the people around them to love God and His Word.

As my kids get older, they are spending an increasing amount of time away from Kari and me. School. Friends. Athletic teams. I know that as the years go by this trend will only increase.

Thankfully, many of their friends love Jesus. And yet, several come from homes of different faith backgrounds – or no faith at all. Kari and I have no desire to isolate our kids from any relationships with non-believers. After all, we do want them to *"go into all the world and make disciples!"* (Mt. 28)

And so we pray. We pray that their friends who already know Jesus would be strengthened in their faith and their own love for God's Word. We pray that their friends who don't know Jesus would come to know Him and the joy and peace that knowing Him brings. We pray that our kids and their friends would *"administer God's grace in its various forms"* (I Peter 4:10) in their schools, on their teams, with their friends, and throughout our neighborhood.

Pray for protection.

There is one last element of this principle we need to address before wrapping up this chapter. It is something we don't talk about very frequently in our homes and churches. It has to do with the opposition.

Put clearly: The next generation has an enemy. You have an enemy. Your children have an enemy. The students in your youth group have an enemy. The adorable, innocent kids in your Sunday school classes have an enemy.

I am not trying to over-dramatize this, but all throughout the Bible, God takes the devil pretty seriously. We rarely do. Take a look at these words from the end of Peter's first letter:

> Be self-controlled and alert. Your enemy the devil prowls around like a roaring lion looking for someone to devour. (I Peter 5:8)

All too often, we talk generically about the "impact of culture" or "peer pressure." Don't get me wrong, these are important topics and need to be discussed and addressed. But rarely do we talk about the *specific attack* our kids and students are under by the one who seeks to deceive them and destroy them. Rarely do we remind our kids that the devil is prowling around. Rarely do we remind them that he is trying to devour them. Yes, it sounds harsh. And it is exactly that *harshness* that should jolt us into praying fervently for the next generation!

If someone were trying to *physically* harm one of my kids, it would not take any thought whatsoever to determine whether I would help them. Of course I would instantly fight back! I wouldn't stop fighting off the attacker until my kids were either safe or I was dead.

The last thing the devil wants is for the next generation to be in the habit of regularly entering into and developing a relationship with God through His Word. He knows how dangerous that is! And so he is on the attack. And his attack is on many levels from many angles.

Praying for your children or students is the most effective way to combat this. The stakes are simply too high not to pray.

A prayer for your children and students

Lord Jesus, I pray that _____ would fall in love with Your Word. May Your Father draw them to You. (John 6:44) May they hide Your Word in their hearts, that they might not sin against You. (Ps 119:11) May they meditate on it day and night, so that they may be careful to do everything written in it. (Joshua 1:8) Protect them from the attacks of the devil. (I Peter 5:8) And may they say along with David, "Oh, how I love your law! I meditate on it all day long." (Ps 119:97)

---

[1]Check out *Praying the Scriptures for Your Children/Teenagers* by Jodie Berndt and *The Power of a Praying Parent* by Stormie Omartian as a good starting point.

Your own ideas for putting Principle Six into practice...

Principle Seven:

Read it together.

"Children are made readers on the laps of their parents."
—Emilie Buchwald

"Some books are to be tasted, others to be swallowed, and some few to be chewed and digested: that is, some books are to be read only in parts, others to be read, but not curiously, and some few to be read wholly, and with diligence and attention."
—Francis Bacon

"Yes, the Bible is the Word of Almighty God. But it also happens to be a jolly good read."
—Anonymous

I can hear some of you saying, "Seriously? Read it together? That's a little obvious, don't you think?" Yes. It is. I also know my own tendency to forget to do it. So maybe I am writing this chapter as a personal kick in the backside. And maybe you too are someone who forgets the importance of slowing down, sitting your kid on your lap (or at least somewhere in the room if the whole lap thing could cause injury), picking up the Bible, and simply reading it together.

The more I think about it, the more it seems that the simple act of reading it together is the foundation on which most of the other principles rest. When we read it together we will love it more. When we read it together we will talk about it. When we read it together we will be much more likely to take it with us into "real life." When we read it together... (Ok, you get the point.)

As I mentioned earlier in this book, part of my preparation for writing was to solicit stories from other parents, youth pastors, and children's pastors about how they were helping the next generation fall in love with God's Word. The responses came from people of different ages, backgrounds, parts of the country, and even from overseas. And while the responses varied in content and ideas, there was one thread that I found in almost every one: They read it together.

> There is just something that happens when we read together that doesn't happen any other way.

There is just something that happens when we read together that doesn't happen any other way. Even when my kids and I are reading a book other than the Bible, there is a special connection that is hard to explain. Conversations just...well...start. Questions are asked. Topics get brought up. Creativity is unleashed.

Read it together.

How much more profound when the centerpiece of that connection, those conversations, the questions, and the creativity is the Living Word of God!

Here are just a handful of the responses I received:

- My 13-year old daughter and I read together, out loud, and when we get done with a book of the Bible we discuss it. She asks questions and we have thoughtful discussions about it. It's wonderful! (Eric – Puyallup, WA)
- One thing I have done with my own children (nine-year-old twins) since the day they came home from the hospital is to spend time in God's Word over breakfast each morning. Sometimes it is a children's devotional, and other times we pick a book in the Bible and read a chapter each morning (with expression! So important for children!). (Kim – Gig Harbor, WA)
- There are many times during my daily reading where I'll see something exciting and I'll reread the passage to my son and share with him – on his level – what it means. Sometimes I'll be goofy and make the story fun and sometimes I'll be very serious (depending on the story) and make it like a play as I read in different voices for different characters. He loves that. (Brad – Vancouver, WA)
- My wife and I have started teaching children's church at our church. One thing that we do is write a list of Bible verses that are included in the lesson on the white board. Then we take volunteers to look up and read a verse when we get to it in the lesson. This does keep them more engaged as they aren't just sitting there listening to me talk for 45 minutes. Plus they get to read firsthand that what we are teaching comes directly from God's Word. (Matt – O' Fallon, MO)
- I have a Bible app on my phone and my daughter will sit on my lap and I'll read it to her and make it fun. (RJ – Orting, WA)

Teenagers. Little kids. Home. On the road. Sunday school. Breakfast table. Wherever. Whenever. These people are reading the Bible with the next generation. And they love it.

A Note about HOW We Read

Think about the last time you read the Bible out loud – or heard it read. Maybe you were at home. Most likely it was at church. What was it like? How was it read? Was it engaging? Could you see the characters? Did you picture the scene? Smell the smells? Feel the warmth...or coolness?

If you answered "no" to these questions you are, sadly, in the majority. Most of the times that I have heard the Bible read out loud it wasn't engaging at all. In fact, it was downright boring. Not only are the listeners uninterested, but most of the *readers* are uninterested in what they are reading!

Now think about the last time you read – or had read to you – anything *other* than the Bible. What was that like? Engaging? Could you see the characters? Hear the sounds? Of course you could. Our brains love to paint vivid pictures in our minds. And our brains do it quite easily.

That's why reading a novel before seeing the movie is always a painful experience for me. I can't be the only one who has wondered if a movie's casting director even read the book! *That's not what he looked like! She was taller! He was shorter! She had brown hair! He had no hair!* We wouldn't think these things if we hadn't painted a clear picture of these people in our brains as we read. So why is it when we read the Bible we rarely have that same experience?

When I teach a *Falling in Love with God's Word Workshop*[1] I address this very issue. A huge part of the problem rests on one word: *expectation.* Most of us don't expect the Bible to be engaging. We expect it to be true. We expect to learn something (sometimes). But we don't expect to laugh. We don't expect to get "lost" in the story. We don't expect the characters to leap off the page. And expectation is vital to enjoyable, engaging reading.

As we read with the next generation, we first have to raise our own level of expectation. After all, the Bible was written by the Author of Life, the Creator of Creativity, and the Inventor of Stories! Then we must let that expectation lead to reading that is filled with energy, passion, and bringing the story to life for the listener.

Read it together.

> ### Read the Bible like you are reading Curious George©
> ### to a five-year-old.

Put it this way: Have you ever read *Curious George©* to a five-year-old? How did you do it? Did the Man with the Yellow Hat sound just like George? Did George sound just like the grocery store owner, or the neighbor, or the zookeeper? Of course not. Did you slow your reading down during the part about George meandering through the forest? Did you speed up as the books in the library, or the groceries, or the sporting equipment came crashing down? Of course. You didn't think about it. You just did it.

So why don't we read the Bible the same way? I have said to many people, "Read the Bible like you are reading *Curious George©* to a five-year-old. Change the volume. Change the pace. Give the characters voices. After all, they didn't sound like the monotone voice you are reading with now!" When we read the Bible in a dry, monotone voice and everything else with energy and passion, we are subtly telling the next generation that the Bible is something we *should* study and read, but it is not very enjoyable. Nothing could be further from the truth!

Try this exercise. With an attitude of expectation, read the following ten verses from the Gospel of John out loud – as if you were reading to a five-year-old:

> *When it was almost time for the Jewish Passover, Jesus went up to Jerusalem. In the temple courts he found men selling cattle, sheep and doves, and others sitting at tables exchanging money. So he made a whip out of cords, and drove all from the temple courts, both sheep and cattle; he scattered the coins of the money changers and overturned their tables. To those who sold doves he said, "Get these out of here! How dare you turn my Father's house into a market!" His disciples remembered that it is written: "Zeal for your house will consume me."*
>
> *Then the Jews then demanded of him, "What miraculous sign can you show us to prove your authority to do all this?"*
>
> *Jesus answered them, "Destroy this temple, and I will raise it again in three days."*

The Jews replied, "It has taken forty-six years to build this temple, and you are going to raise it in three days?" But the temple he had spoken of was his body. After he was raised from the dead, his disciples recalled what he had said. Then they believed the Scripture and the words that Jesus had spoken. (John 2:13-22)

How was it? Different than the last time you read this story? Think through that story one more time and view the scene with your mind's eye. (I can't remember ever seeing animals for sale at my church.) Hear with your mind's ear. (The noise of the animals. The crack of the whip.) Smell with your mind's nose. (Oops, sorry about that. I feel like I am at the County Fair.)

While this is a story with characters, locations, and animals, the same principle applies to any other section of the Bible. When you read Philippians, think about how you would read a letter from a dear friend whom you haven't seen in a few years. Now imagine that the letter started out with the words *I thank my God every time I remember you.* That's a letter I would devour – not just "get through."

Closing Thought

I will end this chapter with something I heard someone say well over a decade ago. I can't remember who said it, or the context in which I heard it, but I'll never forget what was said:

Two thousand years ago God gave us His Living Word. And we've spent the last 2000 years trying to kill it!

That may sound harsh, but my experience in how I read the Bible for the first 20 years of my life – and how I frequently hear it read today – tells me that it is pretty spot on. Our job is not to give life to the Bible and make it interesting. The life is already there. It already *is* interesting! We just need to keep that in mind as we read and then let that life flow out of our mouths and into the ears of our children and students. They will love it. We will love it. And all of us will grow in our love for God and His beautiful, engaging, passionate Word.

---

[1] *Falling in Love with God's Word* is a workshop I teach for churches based on my first book of the same title. For more information about hosting a workshop visit www.thatyoumayknow.com and look under "Speaking."

Your own ideas for putting Principle Seven into practice...

Principle Eight:

Get creative with it.

"Creativity is inventing, experimenting, growing, taking risks, breaking rules, making mistakes, and having fun."

—Mary Lou Cook

"Creativity is contagious. Pass it on."

—Albert Einstein

"Every child is an artist. The problem is how to remain an artist once he grows up."

—Pablo Picasso

Like Ice Cream

A glass of water. A banana nut muffin. One-man drama. A comedy video. Words fading in and out on a screen. The last scene of a movie. A guitar. A young woman painting on stage. Two pictures of an outhouse. A white board. A clown costume. A hike. A mansion. An imaginary girl named Samantha Small.

What do all these have in common? I have used every one of them in my attempt to help the next generation fall in love with God's Word. Some were simple. Some were elaborate. Some were born out of a crazy idea in my head. Some had their genesis in a group discussion. Some were used in a church setting. Some were used near a mountain lake. The message of this chapter is extremely simple:

To help the next generation fall in love with God's Word we must get creative.

This does not mean that young people won't respond to a simple, heartfelt reading of a Bible story. (Remember Principle Seven?) It just means that reading is not the only method we use to teach and engage the next generation.

> The key is creativity. The foundation upon which the creativity builds is the Bible. The foundation doesn't change. The truth doesn't change. Delivery does. It has to.

Back to the ice cream analogy for a moment. I am perfectly fine with a scoop of vanilla. (Just had one last night as a matter of fact.) After all, a scoop of vanilla – or three! – is the starting point for most good sundaes. But I don't want a scoop of vanilla every time. Truth be told, I don't even want the same type of ice cream sundae every time. Sometimes I want hot fudge, whipped cream, nuts, and cherries. Sometimes I want chocolate, peanut butter, and bananas. Sometimes I want caramel and almonds. Sometimes I want it in a waffle cone. Sometimes I want it in a bowl... a big bowl!

The key is creativity. The foundation upon which the creativity builds is the Bible. The foundation doesn't change. The truth doesn't change. Delivery changes. It has to. Creative exploring, reading, teaching and experiencing the Bible plants us – and our kids and students – deeply in God's amazing story.

I ended the last chapter by pointing out that we don't need to somehow *make* the Bible exciting. The Bible is exciting already! Creativity helps us *remember* that excitement and *retain* what we read and hear.

We have all heard the statistics about the effect that seeing, hearing, and doing have on learning. In case you haven't I will give you one quick example. There was a study done in the mid-90's called the Weiss-McGrath Report. The focus was on juror retention when evidence was presented verbally, visually, or both. They found that after 72 hours, participants retained only 10% of evidence presented *verbally*. Those who received the information *visually* retained 20%. Here's the kicker: Those who both heard and saw the evidence retained 65% of the information! Now...I'm no math genius, but that's an increased retention rate of 650% over simply hearing it!

So many of our "devotional" times, Sunday school classes, and youth groups are designed to present information verbally. Kids sit there. Adults talk. We wonder why they don't care or remember. According to Weiss and McGrath, if all we are trying to do is get information in kids' heads, then we would actually be better off letting them just sit and read it themselves. At least that would be visual presentation and they would remember 20% instead of 10%!

Please know that my desire is not to bash what people are doing, but help us all recognize the seriousness of the situation and the need for creativity. I also pray that you don't get discouraged, thinking *"Keith is saying I need to completely overhaul everything I am doing. I don't have the time, resources, or energy."* I am more interested in the next small step than a complete overhaul.

Like Ice Cream

So what is **one thing** you can do with your next youth group talk, Sunday school lesson, or family devotional? Even if it is simply holding a basket with five pieces of bread and two cans of tuna fish while you tell the story of Jesus feeding several thousand people, your students will be 650% more likely to remember what you tell them. Start simple. Creativity begets creativity.

While adding visual creativity to any teaching will have a tremendous effect on learning and enjoyment, a vast majority of the youth pastors, children's pastors and parents I heard from talked about creative ways in which they have their children and students *interact* as part of the learning process. Here is a sample of what I heard:

- One family shared how acting the Bible stories out had become a regular part of their family time in God's Word. The mom wrote, *"The Good Samaritan was a favorite...probably because of the brotherly pummeling that could happen as part of the story!"* Nice.
- One man wrote that he has people read I Corinthians 13 out loud inserting their own name whenever they see the word "love." Then they discuss whether the way Paul described what love is would also describe their own actions and attitudes.
- A mom created an advent calendar that had a Bible verse inserted into each day. She chose verses that not only told the Christmas story, but many of them were verses she could insert her kids' names into. *For God so loved Nathan that He sent...* (She was actually combining Principle Eight with Principles Four and Seven!)
- I heard from two different people from opposite ends of the country who wrote of how powerful and effective the puppet ministries have become at their churches.
- One guy would challenge his youth group and read out only part of a Bible verse. Kids would compete against each other in finding the reference and completing the verse, and have lots of fun in the process.
- Several people wrote of the power of music as a way to be immersed in – and internalize – God's Word. Some were people who still had Scripture songs they learned as a child running

through their heads. Others spoke of writing music with children in their youth groups. One worship leader put many word-for-word Scripture passages to music and her church now sings some of those songs.

The beautiful thing about creativity is that simple and elaborate are both effective. And there is no end to the variety of ways we can engage the next generation – and ourselves for that matter – with God's Word. If you can have students act out the stories themselves – or paint, draw, or sculpt the stories – they will remember it. It will be real. Not to mention it will be heaps of fun!

For those of you who can't imagine coming up with idea after idea... you are in luck. There are thousands of really creative people who are willing to share.[1] Some of those people are in your family or your church. And some have made a career of putting creative ideas and activities into the hands of parents, school teachers, and ministry workers.

> "Be INTERACTIVE! Can't say that loud enough!"
> -Kim (retired Children's Pastor and
> preschool director)

I have seen this firsthand at our church. Several years ago, we spent the weeks leading up to Easter having our children's ministry area (which is one wing of the Junior High School we meet in) transformed into a Jerusalem Marketplace.[2] People were in costume. There were sets and props. You could mill around and see what was for sale. On Easter morning one of the volunteers – playing the role of a rabbi who was skeptical of Jesus's resurrection – thought he was going to get his clock cleaned by a nine-year-old girl who was out to convince him Jesus was alive. Talk about engaged!

Did it take work? Of course it did. Did we have to come up with all the ideas on our own? Absolutely not. However, that experience is still talked about a few years later by kids and adults alike. And since then, many of our own ideas have come from seeing what *could be*. Our church's

Like Ice Cream

Christmas program is almost always written by people in our own church. No professional script writers. Just people passionate about finding creative ways to engage people with God and His Word.

Let me wrap up Principle Eight by telling you about a church that has taken the simple concept of Scripture internalization and creatively turned it into something that has a powerful effect on the entire church community. The church is St. Michael's Lutheran Church in Bloomington, MN.

Over the last five years or so, I have spoken during a few of their worship gatherings and shared my *Falling in Love with God's Word Workshop* there a few times as well. In the fall of 2008 I received a phone call from Jane Horn – the worship director at St. Michael's. Our conversation went something like this:

> **Jane:** *Hey Keith, you'll never believe what's happening at St. Mike's.*
> **Me:** *I'm listening.*
> **Jane:** *In 2009, we're going to do a year-long sermon series looking at 57 of the most influential chapters in the Bible.[3]*
> **Me:** Ok. (All the while thinking: *Hmmm...sounds like a long series.*)
> **Jane:** *I was talking with the gal who leads our drama team and I said, "What if we had different people internalize the various chapters and share them from memory each time we got together." She said, "Great idea, Jane, but our drama ministry only has 12 people." I told her God would provide the people.*
> **Me:** *Sounds great. Are you going to do it?*
> **Jane:** *Absolutely. In fact, we started taking signups already and people are coming out of the woodwork to participate.*
> **Me:** *You've got to keep me posted!*

Well, Jane kept me posted. By the start of 2009, they had all the slots full. And there was even a waiting list in case people backed out (no one did)! The coolest part for me is that a good number of the people were under the age of 18. It was beautiful.

At some point in *every service*, the curtains would come down over the windows and all the lights would turn out. It was too dark to read. A spotlight would shine a beam of light to a spot on the stage. And someone would begin to speak the Word of God from memory. With passion.

With emotion. And hundreds of people would listen to God's Word in awestruck silence.

In September that year I had the chance to go and meet with some of the presenters. That weekend I found out that very few of the presenters throughout the year were – or had ever been – on the drama team. There was an elementary school girl and one of the 20-something volunteers who shared a chapter of Jeremiah. A father used the words of the Bible to describe the building of the temple. A mom shared the amazing worship scene of Isaiah 6. Two teenage boys lived out Saul's conversion in Acts 9. A young woman shared the last chapter of Revelation. A man nearly 90 years old shared I Corinthians 13. An entire family shared parts of Matthew 28, and by the end the kids were all sitting at their father's feet as he said, "*Therefore, go and make disciples...*" Powerful!

> ## They were cheering for the Word of God!

The moment that almost brought me to tears came on Sunday morning. I was asked to share the chapter for that day. Before I began, I asked the congregation how they have been enjoying hearing the Word of God. I never could have expected what happened next. They broke into raucous applause. Even a bit of hooting and hollering. I thought I was at the Vikings game that was still a couple hours from kick-off! They were *cheering* for the Word of God. It was truly one of the most beautiful moments I have had in ministry thus far.[4]

Remember what I said several paragraphs ago: Creativity starts with *the next step*. It is not about the complete overhaul. One step. One idea. One new illustration. One piece of art. One video clip. One song. In the words of Helen Keller:

I cannot do everything, but still I can do something; and because I cannot do everything I will not refuse to do the something that I can do.

Take that next creative step. Today.

[1]Try typing "creative ways to teach the Bible" into Bing.com or Google.com. You will find more ideas, games, illustrations, books, and resources than you know what to do with.

[2]Jerusalem Marketplace is a 5-week, interactive, immersive curriculum put out by Group Publishing.

[3]In the Lutheran Calendar there are 57 "gatherings" with the extra times like Maundy Thursday, Good Friday, etc.

[4]I recently spoke to Jane Horn and this practice of presenting internalized Scripture at every service has continued to this day. And they have no intention of ever stopping! Lovely.

Your own ideas for putting Principle Eight into practice...

Principle Nine:

Make it a priority.

"*The key is not to prioritize what's on your schedule, but to schedule your priorities.*"

—Stephen Covey

"*Listen, my sons, to a father's instruction; pay attention and gain understanding. I give you sound learning, so do not forsake my teaching. For I too was a son to my father, still tender, and cherished by my mother. Then he taught me, and he said to me, "Take hold of my words with all your heart; keep my commands, and you will live.*"

—Proverbs 4:1-4

"*We make time for what is important...and excuses for the rest.*"

—Anonymous

There is a nagging question running through my head: *How do I write a chapter on making the Bible a priority without making it feel like a guilt trip for those who haven't?*

Truth be told, I am not sure that I can. As I have said earlier, the last thing I want is for people to read this book and come away feeling guilty about their parenting or the way they run their children's ministry or youth program. However, there have certainly been many times in my life when someone has called out something of importance and God has used that little twinge of guilt to spur me on to action.

> I can't think of anything that I have ever done well or learned thoroughly that I hadn't first made a priority.

The bottom line is that I can't think of anything that I have ever done well or learned thoroughly that I hadn't first made a priority. What can we get good at without spending time doing it? What can we learn without spending time studying it? What relationship can we build without spending time investing in it?

We intuitively *know* that for our kids – and us! – to love God's Word, we have to make it a priority. But with the busyness of life, we somehow *hope* that it will "just happen." Sadly, this is almost never the case.

So...where do we start? Just like with Principle One, the first step is to make an honest evaluation of where the Bible fits into your current priority list. How is the Bible being woven into your life at home? How are you engaging the students in your youth group with the Bible? How are your Sunday school teachers bringing the Bible to life for the kids in their classes? Do you ever talk about the Bible while you are in the car (even if it means taking the unthinkable step of turning off the radio!)?

Make it a priority.

Time

To be clear: This is not just a *time* issue. Time is only one indicator of priorities. I firmly believe that looking at "time spent" is much more valuable when looking *back* than when looking *ahead*. If you look back at the previous week or month, there will certainly be some value in assessing how much time you spent reading the Bible, discussing it, or finding creative ways to weave the truths of Scripture into everyday life. If the time you spent was nonexistent or very minimal, that should certainly be a red flag.

However, we often take the "time spent" method and use it to prescribe what our day, week, or month should look like. *We will spend 30 minutes doing this Bible activity. We will go to church for 90 minutes once a week. We will have small group every other Tuesday evening.*

What happens when you miss something in that scenario? Talk about guilt! When we reduce falling in love with God's Word to items on our To Do List, we set ourselves up for failure. This approach also removes the *relational* component for our interaction with God through His Word. Remember: The goal is to help the next generation fall in love with God and His Word, not just know it in their heads.

I understand that this is a bit of a sticky issue. On the one hand I am saying we need to make the Bible a priority. On the other I am saying to not make it *just about the time* spent doing the activities that typically indicate that something is a priority. This is one of those gray areas that isn't as neat and clean as we would like it to be. Bottom line: Use time as an *evaluator*, not just a prescriber.

Mindset

A huge piece of this puzzle is *mindset*. Am I doing what I am doing to build a relationship with God, or to somehow win His approval? Let's take a look at a real-life example and see if this issue becomes a bit clearer.

You decide you are going to read your kids something from the Bible each night before bed. Certainly sounds like a good idea.

In Scenario A, you find a story, read it, close your Bible, say your prayers, turn off the light, and head out of the room. In Scenario B, you find a story, read it (with emotion!), ask your kids about it, share some thoughts of your own, see how the idea from the story fits into what they did that day or what they are facing the next, pray (specifically), turn off the light, and head out of the room.

Both are activities you can "check off" on your To Do List. However, they are done with very different mindsets, and as a result, have very different outcomes. Scenario A is done with a mindset of this-is-something-I-should-do. Scenario B is done with an attitude of this-will-build-our-relationship-with-God-and-each-other.

Effort

In the above scenarios, the second one certainly takes more effort. And maybe that is the easiest way to understand what I mean by making it a priority. We put effort, thought, and energy into things that are priorities for us. We can certainly "check off" activities that are not priorities, but simply need to get done. Did the laundry. *Check.* Scheduled the bus for the youth retreat. *Check.* Put together the volunteer list for Sunday school snacks. *Check.* Read the Bible. *Check.* (Oops...didn't mean to put that one on the list.)

> "I just don't think there's any substitute for mom and dad prioritizing that time with the kids."
> —Nicole (mother)

I have no intention of misleading anyone into thinking that helping the next generation fall in love with God's Word is easy. It requires a lot of effort! Of course, I can't think of very many things that are of great value that require no effort. I also can't think of anything more valuable than instilling in my children – and all children – a love for God and His Word.

Make it a priority.

This principle of making it a priority – and the effort that requires – is woven in and around all the other principles. It takes effort to fall in love with the Bible ourselves. It takes effort to read it, talk about it, and bring it into real-life situations. It takes effort to be creative. I don't want to skirt the issue, but rather, tackle it head on: Does it take effort? Yes. Is it worth it? Without a doubt.

Your own ideas for putting Principle Nine into practice...

Final Thoughts

Like Ice Cream

Last Thursday I wrapped up the chapter on Principle Nine (Make it a priority). Friday morning I headed to the airport for a quick, weekend trip to speak at two churches in Minneapolis. Two days later, as I drove to the airport for the flight home, I was reflecting on the weekend and realized that so much of what happened was confirmation that *Like Ice Cream* is exactly what I should be writing and speaking about right now. Hopefully, these three scenes from the weekend will help you see what I mean.

Scene 1 – Saturday morning

The room held about 45 people who had come to a *Falling in Love with God's Word Workshop.* As I looked around, I was thrilled to see that 10-15 of them were in junior high, high school, and college. The younger people were every bit as engaged as the rest. Listening. Laughing. Asking questions.

I was reminded that the next generation is hungry for what is meaningful and true. I was reminded that they are filled with passion when something comes alive for them. I was reminded that they *want* to know God – and His Word. I was reminded that God weeps when we "older folks" bore the next generation into walking away from their faith. I was reminded why I started writing this book in the first place.

Scene 2 – Saturday afternoon

After the workshop, I grabbed some burgers with two of the young people from Scene 1. The guy is a freshman in college. The gal is a senior in high school. Both love Jesus. Both have memorized quite a bit of Scripture. Neither felt like they had "internalized" very much of it.

At one point she said, "I have memorized six books of the Bible. But knowing, understanding, and loving it weren't part of the process. I feel like this puts a whole new layer on it. I am so excited!"

They talked about how they were going to internalize Colossians – together. She shared about possibly presenting Colossians or Ruth during

94

one of the chapels at her high school. He started to brainstorm how the other university students in his Campus Crusade for Christ group could hear about this. She talked about exploring how to get *Like Ice Cream* into the hands of people who attend the homeschooling conference held in her city each year. (Wouldn't hurt my feelings!)

Part of the conversation was even about what an internship or apprenticeship could look like with That You May Know Ministries. There is not much that gets me as excited as teenagers who are excited about reading, internalizing, and sharing God's Word.

Scene 3 – Sunday morning

He was about eight years old. I had just shared the book of Jonah with 150 elementary school students (and the story from John 9 of the blind man healed with spit and mud). He held his mom's hand as she perused the table where my books and CDs sat. He had a huge smile on his face as this conversation unfolded:

> **Boy:** *That was so awesome!*
> **Mom** (grinning): *What did you think was "awesome" about it?*
> **Boy:** *Well...it was funny.* (starts to chuckle)
> **Mom:** *What part did you think was funny?*
> **Boy:** *Um...I guess...ALL of it! I loved it all!*

He heard the Bible and *loved* it. He didn't just learn something (although learning something is good). He didn't just believe it was true (although it certainly is). He liked it. He laughed. He talked about it with his mom. In fact, he is the one who *started* the conversation. A kid enjoyed the Bible enough to want to talk about it some more. I could not have been more thrilled.

One scoop at a time...

The perfect ice cream sundae isn't something that you imagine and then – *poof!* – it appears. The perfect sundae is built one scoop at a time. One topping at a time. One cherry at a time.

In the same way, building an environment in which our children and students fall in love with God and His Word is done one step at a time.

Like Ice Cream

Sir Winston Churchill said, "It is a mistake to try to look too far ahead. The chain of destiny can only be grasped one link at a time."

With the few remaining sentences we have together, let me encourage you not to look too far ahead. You don't need to do everything. You need to do something. One thing. The next thing. And then add to it...one more thing.

First, fall in love with the Bible yourself. Then talk about it with your children or students. Make it real for them. Remind them of who it says they are. Surround them with people who love it. Pray about it. Read it with them. Get creative with it. And please, make it a priority.

Now...put this book down, pick up your Bible, sit down with a kid, and get started. Maybe even over a bowl of ice cream.

Appendix 1
A note to parents of older children

I recently had someone say to me, "I have three kids who are out of high school. One is walking with the Lord. One is on the fence. And one is flat-out running away. What would you say to me?" My heart sank as I could see the what-should-I-have-done-differently look in her eyes.

Sadly, I have had several of these types of conversations. Parents who have prayed for their kids for years, only to feel that their kids are further away from Christ than ever. Youth pastors who have "tried everything" only to feel that their students aren't getting it. Well-intentioned parents who spent years believing that getting their kids to youth group and Sunday school *was* making their spiritual life a priority. Parents who came to Christ after their kids were older and wonder what they can do now.

Quite honestly, there is a large part of me that feels like I should step aside and find someone else to write this chapter. After all, my kids are only eight, six, and two! But as I have sat, listened, and shared with these parents and youth pastors, as well as many parents who have seen their adult children come back to the faith, what follows will – I pray – be a few words of encouragement.

Principle Six is forever.

So often we look at prayer as a last resort. In actuality, prayer must always be our first step, our everyday practice, *and* our last resort. I obviously wrote a whole chapter on this, but let me remind you that it is God's responsibility – by His grace and through His Spirit – to draw your children to Himself. (Remember John 6.)

One of our most important jobs as parents is to continually offer our children – no matter what age or circumstance – to God in prayer. Truthfully, I do not believe that all of the prayers we offer on behalf of our children are for *them*. Many times, when our prayers turn to pleas, cries, screams, or heart-broken silence, God reminds us that He is here for *us*.

We don't just pray for God to draw our children. We also pray that God would continue to draw us to Himself. We don't just pray that God would help our children fall in love with His Word. We also pray that He will help us experience the life found in His Living Word. We don't just pray that God would surround our children with people who love Him. We are also reminded as we pray that we are not alone. We don't just pray for the protection of our children. We also pray that God's truth would drown out the lies of the accuser of our souls.

Simply put: God often uses the prayers we speak for our children to remind us that He is with us and for us.

Keep doing what you can do.

Each person reading this has a different scenario when it comes to their children. Some have children at home. Some have kids on the other side of the city...or the globe. Some have wonderful relationships with their kids. Some have a lot of healing that needs to occur.

Let me encourage you to continue to employ the principles in this book as much as your situation allows. This is especially important when it comes to your own relationship with God through His Word, praying for your kids, letting God's Word guide the content of your conversations, and the way His Word is honored, loved, and obeyed in your home.

Your kids might not be receptive to hearing specific verses shared with them, but everyone wants to hear that they are valuable and loved. They might not read the Bible with you, but you can pray those Scriptures over their lives.

As parents, it is vital that we own up to our past mistakes with our children. It is equally vital that we celebrate the successes that we did and do have. Even more important is to remember that God's hand is on each one of our children. As we have talked about several times already, it is God's responsibility to draw them to Himself. God's timing is not our own, yet *He is at work in each of our kids' lives.* We can be hopeful about our children loving God and loving His Word, through praying to and trusting in the God who is sovereign. We must always be mindful that God is a God of redemption and restoration. He knows our past *and* He knows our future. Our job is to accept His mercy, grace, and forgiveness – and press on...with hope. (Romans 15:13)

God is the Perfect Father...
and many of His children rebelled.

Take a look at these words from the very beginning of Isaiah:

> *Hear, O heavens! Listen, O earth!*
> *For the Lord has spoken:*
> *"I reared children and brought them up,*
> but they have rebelled against me.
> *The ox knows his master,*
> *the donkey his owner's manger,*
> but Israel does not know,
> *My people do not understand.*
> —Isaiah 1:2-3

God is perfect. His parenting is perfect. His love is perfect. Every decision He makes regarding His children is for their good. And yet, so many walk away. So many rebel. So many don't even care. He has not forced anyone to love, serve, obey, and glorify Him. He longs for them to want that relationship again – or for the first time.

Does His heart ache and break? Absolutely. Does He understand your discouragement and confusion? Yes. Is He *present* with you in this season of not knowing what "will be" for your children? Most definitely. He has not given up on you. He has not given up on your children. After all, they are not just your children...they are His children too. And He loves them.

Appendix 2
Resources to Get You Started

This is in no way intended to be an exhaustive list of resources. In fact, so many terrific resources and websites are regularly being released and updated, that it would be impossible to keep a printed book current. You can find a more current – and longer! – list in the "Resources" section of www.ThatYouMayKnow.com. And if you have a resource, book, or website that you think would be helpful to share, please send an email to ideas@ thatyoumayknow.com.

Bibles
- *The Beginner's Bible: Timeless Children's Stories* (Zonderkidz, 2005) Ages 2-6
- *The Big Picture Story Bible* by David Helm (Crossway Books, 2010) Ages 2-10
- *The Adventure Bible* (Zonderkidz, 2008) Ages 6-12
- *The Action Bible* (David C. Cook, 2010) Ages 6-14
- *Student's Life Application Bible* (Tyndale House Publishers, Inc., 2006) Ages 12-18
- *NIV Student Bible* (Zondervan, 2008) Ages 12-18

Books
- *Praying the Scriptures for Your Children* by Jodie Berndt (Zondervan, 2001)
- *Praying the Scriptures for Your Teenagers: Discover How to Pray God's Will for Their Lives* by Jodie Berndt (Zondervan, 2007)
- *The Power of a Praying Parent* by Stormie Omartian (Harvest House Publishers, 2007)
- *Visionary Parenting: Capture a God-Sized Vision for Your Family* by Rob Rienow (Randall House Publications, 2009)
- *1001 Ways to Introduce Your Child to the Bible* by Kathie Reimer (B&H Publishing Group, 2002)
- *The Encyclopedia of Bible Crafts for Children* (Group Publishing, Inc., 2002)

- *The Encyclopedia of Bible Crafts for Preschoolers* (Group Publishing, Inc., 2003)
- *The Encyclopedia of Bible Games for Children's Ministry* (Group Publishing, Inc., 2004)
- *Sticky Situations (1 & 2)* by Betsy Schmitt (Tyndale House, 2001 & 2006)
- *TRU Curriculum* from David C. Cook (www.tru.davidccook.com)

Websites

www.thatyoumayknow.com

www.famtime.com

www.ministry-to-children.com

www.childrensministry.com

www.kidology.org

www.cmconnect.org

www.kidzmatter.com

www.egadideas.com

www.studentministry.org

www.simplyyouthministry.com

www.biblegateway.com

www.group.com

www.davidccook.com

www.visionaryparenting.com

About the Author

Keith Ferrin was raised in the church, came to love Jesus at an early age, but didn't really "fall in love" with the Bible until he was in his early 20's. In 1996 he founded That You May Know Ministries – a ministry founded on one principle: *The Living Word of God is a reality, not a phrase.* Since then, he has traveled around the world speaking at churches, conferences, universities, and anywhere else people will let him.

He is the husband of one and the father of three. They live together just outside of Seattle. When he is not writing or speaking, you will find him running around to kids' sporting events, playing in the backyard, hanging out at the lake, sipping coffee...or eating a bowl of ice cream.

Notes, ideas, resources, and prayers...

Notes, ideas, resources, and prayers...

Notes, ideas, resources, and prayers...

Notes, ideas, resources, and prayers...

Made in the USA
Middletown, DE
20 April 2015